ScottForesman ENGLISH
On Your Mark 1

WORKBOOK

ROBERT D. LEE
Pasadena City College
Pasadena, California

DARLEEN A. LENNAN
Commonwealth of the Northern Mariana Islands
Public School System
Saipan

JACQUELINE L. LOVELACE
Dallas Independent School District
Dallas, Texas

MAYRA L. MENENDEZ, ED.S.
The School Board of Broward County
Florida

SERIES CONSULTANTS

JAMES E. PURPURA
Institute of North American Studies
Barcelona, Spain

DIANE PINKLEY
Institute of North American Studies
Badalona, Spain

ScottForesman

Illustrations by Ruta Daugavietis 21, 42, 43 top four pieces, 44, 45, 57, 58, 60, 61, 62, 73, 74, 76, 80; John Faulkner 9, 10, 14, 25, 26, 29, 31, 43 center car, 51, 52, 53, 68, 81, 82, 83, 88; T. R. Garcia: 4, 5, 7, 15, 41, 46, 48, 65, 66, 67, 70, 85, 89, 90, 92, 94; Jared Lee: 17, 18, 20, 23, 24, 33, 34, 36, 37, 49, 50, 54, 55; Christian Musselman: 43 bottom; Jeff Weyer 64, 93.

ISBN: 0-673-19591-0

7 8 9 10-BW-0201009998

PRACTICE 1:
Look at the picture. Circle the word.

desk   (book)   door

1.

pen   name   notebook

2.

address   chalk   eraser

3.

number   letter   line

4.

pencil   picture   paper

5.

circle

chalk   line   circle

6.

desk   chalk   eraser

7.

line   window   letter

PRACTICE 2:
Match. Draw a line.

pen

1. notebook

2. eraser

3. name

4. paper

5. circle

6. letter

7. word

8. chalk

a.

b.

c.

d.

e.

f.

g.

h.

i.

2   UNIT 1   WHAT'S YOUR NAME?

PRACTICE 3:
Listen. Circle the number.

  2   8   (6)

1. 1   3   (9)   2. 7   4   (5)   3. (1) 8   4

4. 5   (2) 10   5. 7   (2) 1   6. 7   (8) 2

7. (3) 9   4   8. 8   3   (6)   9. 3   5   (4)

PRACTICE 4:
Write the number word.

  1 _____one_____

1. 0 _____   2. 5 _____

3. 8 _____   4. 6 _____

5. 2 _____   6. 9 _____

7. 3 _____   8. 10 _____

9. 7 _____   10. 4 _____

PRACTICE 5:
Complete the sentence with the correct number word.

1. Six and one is _____ .

2. Eight and one is _____ .

3. Four and _____ is ten.

4. _____ and three is five.

5. One and _____ is six.

6. _____ and five is eight.

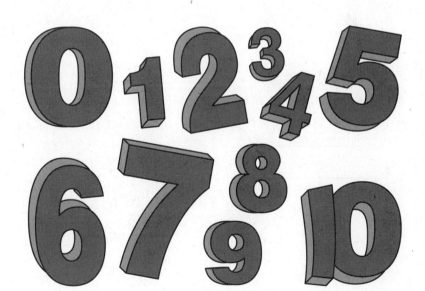

PRACTICE 6:
Listen. Circle the letter.

(p)   f   q

1.   h   r   (e)
2.   g   (j)   y
3.   (n)   w   m
4.   (v)   w   s
5.   h   k   (c)
6.   e   (u)   a
7.   w   (y)   l
8.   (a)   y   e
9.   (x)   z   k
10.   o   (q)   p

PRACTICE 7:
Listen. Write the letter.

_a_

1. _y_   2. _i_   3. _u_   4. _a_   5. _e_

6. _l_   7. _n_   8. _h_   9. _r_   10. _g_

PRACTICE 8:
Listen. Write the word.

your

1. _name_   2. _notebook_
3. _what's_   4. _address_
5. _It's_   6. _page_
7. _door_   8. _pencil_
9. _letter_   10. _desk_

1.

How are you?

What's this?

What's your name?

2.

It's a notebook.

My name is Ed.

Fine, thanks.

3.

It's an eraser.

It's my name.

It's chalk.

PRACTICE 10:
Read. Write the word.

Hi! _____My_____ name is Maria.
        My / Your

1. _____ your name?
   It's / What's

2. _____ name is Yoshi.
   My / Your

3. _____ this?
   It's / What's

4. _____ an eraser.
   It's / What's

5. _____ this?
   It's / What's

6. _____ chalk.
   It's / What's

7. _____ this?
   It's / What's

8. _____ my book.
   It's / What's

 PRACTICE 11:
Listen. Circle the word.

	door	(window)	board
1.	name	number	notebook
2.	eraser	address	desk
3.	page	book	door
4.	pencil	letter	name
5.	book	pen	window
6.	eraser	board	door
7.	circle	pencil	line
8.	name	chalk	book
9.	notebook	name	word
10.	letter	paper	address

PRACTICE 12:
Read about Ken and Rosa. Fill out the form for Rosa.

My first name is Ken.
My last name is Ono.

My first name is Rosa.
My last name is Sánchez.

Name

Ono   _Ken_
Last   **First**

Name

_____
Last   **First**

PRACTICE 13:
Fill out the form about yourself.

Name

_____
Last   **First**

PRACTICE 14:
Write sentences about your first and last names.

_____

_____

Read. Follow the directions.

Draw a line from the **paper** to number **3**.

Draw a line from the **eraser** to number **2**.

Draw a line from the **chalk** to number **5**.

Draw a line from the **notebook** to number **1**.

Draw a line from the letter **b** to number **4**.

Write your first name in number **6**.

Write your last name in number **10**.

Circle number **8**.

Write the number **4** in number **7**.

Count the pencils. Write the number word in number **9**.

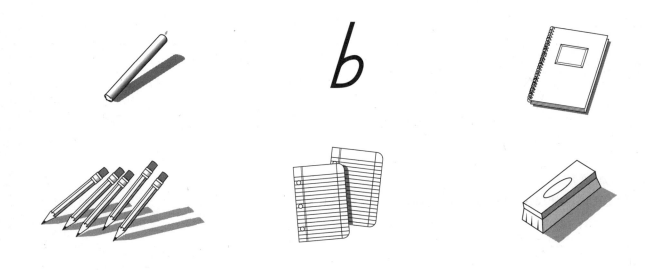

1.	2.	3.	4.	5.
6.	7.	8.	9.	10.

UNIT 2 Where Is It?

PRACTICE 1:
Look at the picture. Circle the word.

number   eraser   (notebook)

1.   circle   table   chair

2.   woman   boy   girl

3.   book bag   book   wastebasket

4.   girl   woman   man

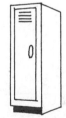
5.   locker   circle   desk

6.   notebook   table   wastebasket

7.   girl   boy   man

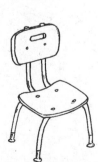
8.   chalk   chair   locker

PRACTICE 2:
Match. Write the letter on the line.

1. _____ book bags

2. _____ wastebasket

3. _____ boys

4. _____ lockers

5. _____ table

6. _____ chairs

7. _____ women

8. _____ girl

9. _____ man

a.

b.

c.

d.

e.

f.

g.

h.

i.

PRACTICE 3:
Listen. Circle the number.

(11)   8   13

1.   14   20   12   2.   19   15   13   3.   20   12   10
4.   16   8   18   5.   17   16   19   6.   13   14   17
7.   10   11   14   8.   17   15   7   9.   19   10   16

PRACTICE 4:
Write the number word.

14   _____fourteen_____

1.   18   _____   2.   20   _____
3.   13   _____   4.   17   _____
5.   11   _____   6.   10   _____
7.   19   _____   8.   15   _____
9.   12   _____   10.   16   _____

PRACTICE 5:
Complete the sentence with the correct number word.

1. Two from fifteen is _____ .

2. Five from sixteen is _____ .

3. Four from _____ is sixteen.

4. _____ from twenty is three.

5. _____ from eighteen is four.

6. Two from _____ is seventeen.

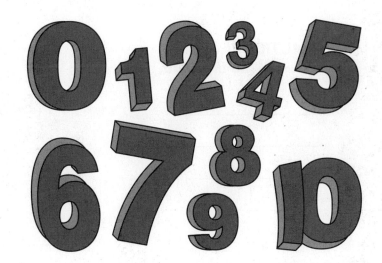

PRACTICE 6:
Listen. Circle the letter.

     (B)   P   T

1.   A   (K)   H
2.   (P)   C   D
3.   E   C   (T)
4.   M   (N)   W
5.   I   (Y)   K
6.   Z   B   (E)
7.   F   (M)   X
8.   (J)   A   K
9.   (Q)   O   C
10. P   B   (R)

PRACTICE 7:
Listen. Write the capital letter.

     A

1. F   2. G   3. O   4. S   5. V
6. U   7. W   8. B   9. H   10. C

PRACTICE 8:
Listen. Write the word.

     table

1. chalk   2. paper
3. woman   4. circle
5. locker   6. desk
7. books   8. notebook
9. girls   10. number

PRACTICE 9:
What's this? What are these? Write the word.

It's   **They're**

_____*It's*_____ a wastebasket.

1. _____ a locker.

2. _____ chairs.

3. _____ a table.

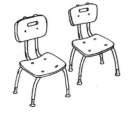
4. _____ books.

 **PRACTICE 10:**
Where's the notebook? Write the word.

in   **on**   **under**

It's _____*on*_____ the chair.

1. It's _____ the book bag.

2. It's _____ the table.

3. It's _____ the locker.

4. It's _____ the desk.

PRACTICE 11:
Listen. Circle the sentence.

~~They're book bags.~~   It's a book bag.

1. It's a wastebasket.   They're wastebaskets.

2. They're chairs.   It's a chair.

3. They're tables.   It's a table.

4. It's a locker.   They're lockers.

5. He's a man.   They're men.

6. They're women.   It's a woman.

PRACTICE 12:
Listen. Circle the answer.

1. It's on the table.   It's under the table.

2. It's in the desk.   It's on the desk.

3. It's under the locker.   It's in the locker.

4. It's in the wastebasket.   It's on the wastebasket.

5. It's under the chair.   It's on the chair.

6. It's on the book bag.   It's in the book bag.

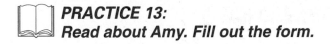

PRACTICE 13:
Read about Amy. Fill out the form.

Her name is Amy Chin.

Her address is 869 Mar Vista Avenue, Dallas, Texas 75211.

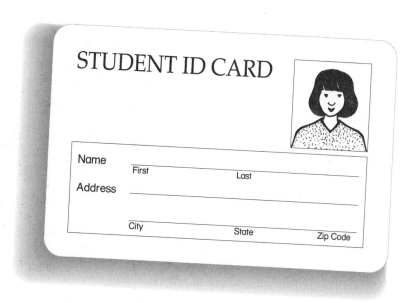

PRACTICE 14:
Write sentences about Abdul.

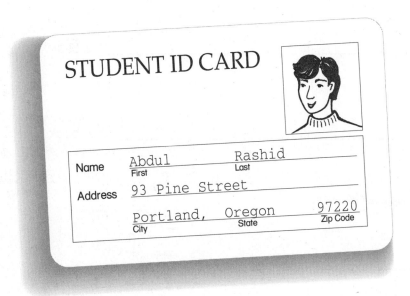

_____

_____

A. Look at the picture. Look at the words. Write the correct word on the line.

| book bag | paper | wastebasket | in | under |
| locker | pencils | book | on | |

1. This is a _____ .

2. The _____ is _____ the desk.

3. The _____ is _____ the table.

4. The _____ are _____ the desk.

5. The _____ is _____ the chair.

6. The _____ is _____ the book.

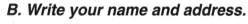

B. Write your name and address.

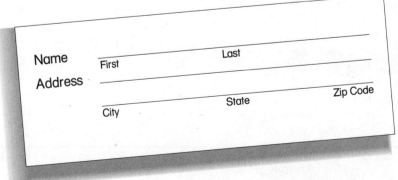

Name _____
First   Last

Address _____

City   State   Zip Code

PRACTICE 1:

Look at the picture. Circle the word.

1.   library   cafeteria   office

2.   class   rest room   gym

3.   library   gym   cafeteria

4.   office   rest room   class

5.   gym   library   office

6.   rest room   office   class

PRACTICE 2:
Match. Write the letter on the line.

1. _____ It's the gym.

a.

2. _____ She's the librarian.

b.

3. _____ It's the office.

c.

4. _____ He's the principal.

d.

5. _____ It's the cafeteria.

e.

6. _____ She's a student.

f.

7. _____ It's the rest room.

g.

PRACTICE 3:
Listen. Circle the number.

1.	20	30	60	**2.**	42	52	82
3.	86	36	46	**4.**	31	91	81
5.	51	56	66	**6.**	93	23	73
7.	47	77	52	**8.**	67	37	27
9.	89	29	39	**10.**	64	74	54

PRACTICE 4:
Write the number word.

20 _____*twenty*_____

1. 70 _____   **2.** 90 _____

3. 80 _____   **4.** 62 _____

5. 44 _____   **6.** 38 _____

7. 56 _____   **8.** 22 _____

9. 81 _____   **10.** 93 _____

PRACTICE 5:
Complete the sentence with the correct number word.

1. Twenty-eight and four is ____*32*_____ .

2. Seventy-six and five is _____ .

3. Nine from fifty-seven is _____ .

4. Sixty-five and _____ is eighty-six.

5. Seven from _____ is thirty-four.

6. _____ and twenty is sixty-two.

PRACTICE 6:
Write the word on the line.

He's   She's

1. _____ a cashier.

2. _____ a librarian.

3. _____ a gym teacher.

4. _____ a principal.

5. _____ a teacher.

6. _____ a student.

PRACTICE 7:
Match. Draw a line.

1. He's   What is

2. She's   He is

3. Who's   It is

4. What's   She is

5. Where's   Where is

6. It's   Who is

PRACTICE 8:
Listen. Write the phone number.

1. Library: _____

2. Mrs. Chen: _____

3. Principal's Office: _____

4. Gloria: _____

5. Parker School: _____

6. Mr. García: _____

7. Gym: _____

8. Ted: _____

PRACTICE 9:
Ask five students. Write their names. Write their phone numbers.

Name: _____ Phone Number: _____

Name: _____ Phone Number: _____

Name: _____ Phone Number: _____

Name: _____ Phone Number: _____

Name: _____ Phone Number: _____

Chen, Tina 555–9826
   1900 Lake Street
Halsted, Diane 136–7491
   634 Clark Street
Johnson, Gloria..................555–3818
   1245 School Street
Lu, Peter 184–3890
   546 Wood Street
Mendoza, Jorge..................274–7274
   690 Beach Drive
Sánchez, Mario 555–2648
   6237 Buena Vista

1. What's Peter's address?

_____

2. What's Ms. Halsted's phone number?

_____

3. What's Gloria's phone number?

_____

4. What's Tina's address?

_____

5. What's Mario's phone number?

_____

6. What's Mr. Mendoza's address?

_____

7. What's Gloria's address?

_____

PRACTICE 11:

Read Mario's ID card. Write about his name, address, and phone number.

Name _Mario_ _Sánchez_
        First   last
Address _6237 Buena Vista_

Miami, Florida 33156
  city   State   Zip Code
Phone Number _(305)555-2648_
              Area Code

His name _____

_____

_____

_____

A. Look at the pictures. Complete the sentences with the correct words.

cafeteria	cashier	librarian	library
office	P.E. teacher	principal	student	teacher

1. My name is Mayka Lu. I'm a _____ . I study English.

2. My name is Mr. Brown. I'm a _____ . I teach math.

3. My name is Mrs. Díaz. I'm a _____ . I work in the _____ .

4. My name is Ms. Lee. I'm a _____ . I work in the _____ .

5. My name is Mr. Marzo. I'm a _____ . I work in the _____ .

cafeteria

Mrs. Díaz

library

Mr. Marzo

Ms. Lee

office

Mayka Lu

Mr. Brown

B. Read about Mayka. Fill out the student ID card for her.

My name is Mayka Lu. My phone number is (608) 111–4392. My address is 245 Maple Avenue, Madison, Wisconsin 53704.

PARKER SCHOOL

STUDENT ID CARD
Student Number 936-87-3781

Name	First _____ Last _____
Address	_____
	City _____ State _____ Zip Code _____
Phone	(___) _____
	Area Code

PRACTICE 1:
Look at the picture. Circle the word.

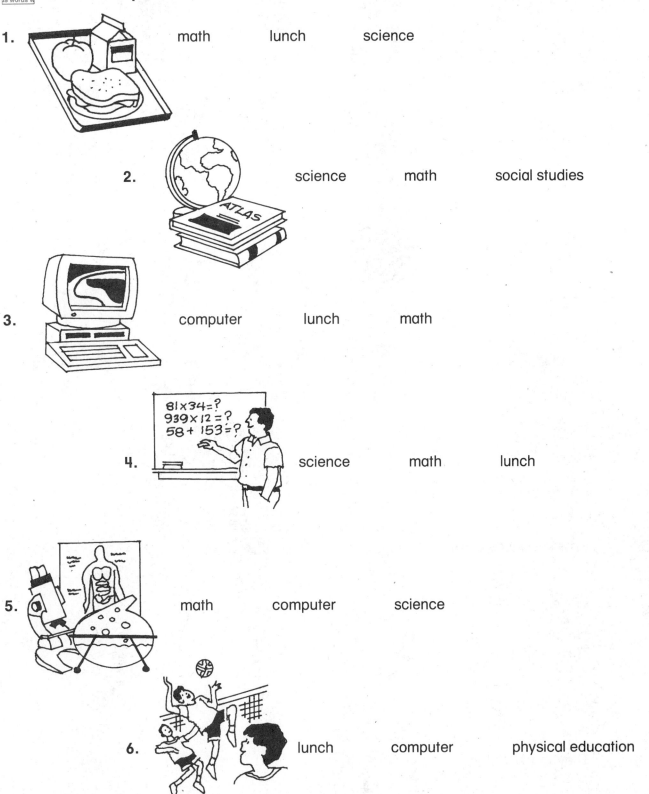

1.   math   lunch   science

2.   science   math   social studies

3.   computer   lunch   math

4.   science   math   lunch

5.   math   computer   science

6.   lunch   computer   physical education

PRACTICE 2:
Match. Write the letter on the line.

a.

b.

c.

d.

e.

f.

1. _____ He's in computer class.

2. _____ He's in science class.

3. _____ She's in social studies class.

4. _____ They're at lunch.

5. _____ She's in math class.

6. _____ They're in P.E. class.

PRACTICE 3:
Listen. Circle the clock with the time you hear.

1. a. 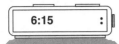 6:15 b.  6:51 ✓

2. a. ✓ b.

3. a.  4:30 ✓ b.

4. a.   b.  5:45 ✓

5. a. 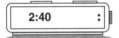 2:40 b.  ✓

6. a. 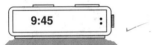 9:45 ✓ b.

7. a.   b. 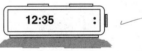 12:35 ✓

8. a.  8:10 ✓ b.

9. a.  2:22 ✓ b.

10. a.   b. 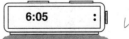 6:05 ✓

PRACTICE 4:
Put the time on the clocks.

It's ten after four.

1. It's half-past one.

2. It's three fifteen.

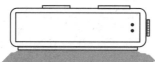

3. It's a quarter to eight.

4. It's nine fifteen.

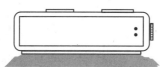

5. It's three fifty-five.

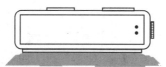

6. It's ten after two.

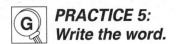

PRACTICE 5:
Write the word.

have   **has**

1. We _____ math class at different times.

2. I _____ math class at 8:30.

3. Javier _____ it at 10:15.

4. Susan _____ it at 12:15.

5. They _____ computer class at 1:00.

6. I _____ computer class at 2:00.

PRACTICE 6:
Write the word. Complete sentence 5 about yourself.

do   **does**

1. Where _____ they _____ their homework?

2. Abdul _____ his homework at home.

3. Elena _____ her homework in the library.

4. When _____ you _____ your homework?

5. I _____ my homework _____ .

PRACTICE 7:
Write the word.

do   **does**   **have**   **has**

1. A: When _____ you _____ English class?

   B: I _____ it at 9:30.

2. A: Where _____ Sandy _____ science class?

   B: She _____ it in Room 12.

3. A: When _____ the students _____ lunch?

   B: They _____ lunch at 11:45.

PRACTICE 8:
Listen. Write the time.

<u>6:30</u>

1. _____   2. _____

3. _____   4. _____

5. _____   6. _____

7. _____   8. _____

PRACTICE 9:
Read Gino's schedule. Answer the questions. Write sentences.

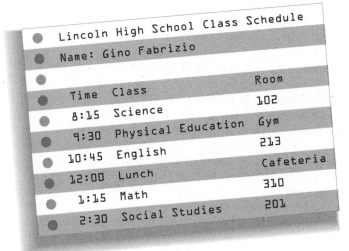

Lincoln High School Class Schedule

Name: Gino Fabrizio

Time	Class	Room
8:15	Science	102
9:30	Physical Education	Gym
10:45	English	213
12:00	Lunch	Cafeteria
1:15	Math	310
2:30	Social Studies	201

1. What time does Gino have math class?

_____

2. What time does he have physical education?

_____

3. What class does Gino have at 10:45?

_____

4. What time does Gino have science class?

_____

5. What class does Gino have at 2:30?

_____

PRACTICE 10:
Read about Gino. Write about yourself.

My name is Gino Fabrizio. I go to Lincoln High School. I have five classes. At 8:15 I have science class. I have P.E. at 9:30 and English class at 10:45. I go to lunch at 12:00. I have math at 1:15. My social studies class is at 2:30.

_____

_____

_____

_____

_____

_____

_____

_____

A. Read the schedule. Complete each sentence with the correct word or words.

```
   Barton School Class Schedule
   Name: Pablo Reyes

   Time   Class
   8:30   Math
   9:25   English
   10:20  Computer
   11:10  Physical Education
   12:00  Lunch
   12:45  Science
   1:55   Social Science
```

1. Pablo has _____ at 9:25.

2. He has lunch at _____ .

3. He _____ computer class at _____ .

4. He has _____ at 12:45.

5. His last class is _____ .

6. He _____ physical education at _____ .

7. His _____ class is math.

B. Finish writing about Pablo's schedule.

My name is Pablo Reyes. I go to _____ School. I have six classes. At 8:30 I have _____

_____

_____

_____

_____

_____

_____

UNIT 5 A Weekly Schedule

PRACTICE 1:
Look at the picture. Circle the word.

1.    music   art   band

2.    basketball   baseball   soccer

3.   music   art   movies

4.    basketball   band   baseball

5.    basketball   baseball   soccer

6.    park   art   movies

7.    art   band   movies

8.    shopping mall   library   park

PRACTICE 2:

Match. Write the letter on the line.

1. _____ They go to the movies on Saturday.

a.

2. _____ She has baseball practice on Thursday.

b.

3. _____ He has art class at 1:00.

c.

4. _____ They go to the shopping mall after school.

d.

5. _____ He plays basketball on Tuesday.

e.

6. _____ They have music class on Tuesday and Thursday.

f.

7. _____ They have soccer practice at 4:00.

g.

8. _____ They have band practice every day.

h.

PRACTICE 3:
Look at John's schedule for the week. Circle the answer.

Monday   *write to Jack*

Tuesday   *go to band practice*

Wednesday   *go to library*

Thursday   *go to band practice*

Friday   *play soccer*

Saturday   *go to baseball practice*

Sunday   *do homework*

1. John goes to the library on   Monday.

    Wednesday.

2. On Friday he   plays soccer.

    reads a book.

3. On   Sunday   John does his homework.

    Saturday

4. John goes to band practice on   Monday and Wednesday.

    Tuesday and Thursday.

5. On   Wednesday   John writes to Jack.

    Monday

6. On Saturday he   plays soccer.

    plays baseball.

PRACTICE 4:
Write the correct word.

1. Jon and Li _____ busy schedules.
　　　　　　　　　have / has

2. They _____ in a band.
　　　　　　　are / is

3. The band _____ rock music.
　　　　　　　　play / plays

4. They _____ band practice every day.
　　　　　　have / has

5. Sue _____ in the band too.
　　　　　　are / is

6. She _____ to the library after band practice.
　　　　　　go / goes

7. She _____ a lot of books.
　　　　　　read / reads

8. Jon _____ his homework after band practice.
　　　　　　do / does

9. He _____ to music at night.
　　　　listen / listens

10. Jon, Li, and Sue _____ soccer practice on the weekend.
　　　　　　　　have / has

　　　　　　　　　　　　　　　　　　　　　　　　　UNIT 5　A WEEKLY SCHEDULE

PRACTICE 5:
Write sentences about what you do. Use <u>always</u> or <u>never</u>.

have art class on Thursday
I always have art class on Thursday.

1. go to school on Sunday

_____

2. do my homework after school

_____

3. have music class on Tuesday

_____

4. have P.E. on Monday

_____

G
PRACTICE 6:
*Look at your partner's answers for Practice 5.
Write about your partner. Use <u>he</u> or <u>she</u>.*

have art class on Thursday
She always has art class on Thursday.

1. _____

2. _____

3. _____

4. _____

PRACTICE 7:
Listen. Mark the days with an X.

	Sunday	Monday	Tuesday	Wednesday	Thursday	Friday	Saturday
band							
basketball							
football	X						
homework							
library							
soccer							

PRACTICE 8:
Ask three students about what they do on Saturday. Write their names and answers.

Name   **What do you do on Saturday?**

1. _____   _____

2. _____   _____

3. _____   _____

Read Anna's schedule. Write the answers.

Anna's Schedule						
Monday	Tuesday	Wednesday	Thursday	Friday	Saturday	Sunday
go to library	go to art class	play soccer	go to music class	go to art class	go to the shopping mall	do homework

1. When does Anna go to the library? _____

2. What does Anna do on Wednesday? _____

3. When does Anna have art class? _____

4. When does she play soccer? _____

5. When does Anna go to the shopping mall? _____

6. When does she do her homework? _____

PRACTICE 10:
Read about Anna. Write about yourself.

My name is Anna Wong. I am always busy. I go to the library on Monday. I go to art class on Tuesday and Friday. On Wednesday I play soccer. I have music class on Thursday. I always go to the mall on Saturday. I always do my homework on Sunday.

_____

_____

_____

_____

_____

_____

A. Read Lin's schedule for this week. Complete each sentence with the correct word or words.

```
    3  Monday                      7  Friday
    have art class                play soccer after school

    4  Tuesday                     8  Saturday
    go to band practice           go to the shopping mall
                                   go to the movies
    5  Wednesday                   9  Sunday
    go to the library after school   do homework

    6  Thursday
    go to band practice
    go to the library after school
```

1. On _____ Lin has art class.

2. On _____ and _____ she goes to the library after school.

3. On Friday she _____ after school.

4. On _____ she does homework.

5. On Saturday she _____ to the shopping mall and the _____ .

6. On _____ and _____ she goes to band practice.

B. Complete Lin's paragraph about her schedule.

My name is _____ . I have a busy schedule. On Monday _____

_____

_____

_____

PRACTICE 1:
Look at the picture. Circle the word.

 family   mother   daughter

1.   son   father   mother

2.   daughter   son   father

3.   mother   son   daughter

4.   daughter   father   mother

5.   sisters   mothers   brothers

6.   brothers   fathers   sisters

7.   grandmother   grandfather   son

8.   grandfather   mother   father

PRACTICE 2:
Complete the sentence. Write the word.

brother's	husband's	sister's	wife's
daughter's	mother's	son's	

I am Gloria's daughter.

My _____*mother's*_____ name is Gloria.

1. I am Bob's sister.

My _____ name is Bob.

2. I am Jim's wife.

My _____ name is Jim.

3. I am David's mother.

My _____ name is David.

4. I am Claudia's husband.

My _____ name is Claudia.

5. I am Angela's father.

My _____ name is Angela.

6. I am Marta's brother.

My _____ name is Marta.

---

42   UNIT 6   THE FAMILY

PRACTICE 3:
Read the sentence. Write the correct word.

I	he	we
you	she	they
	it	

My name is Miguel. _____*I*_____ go to Flora Vista School.

1. My parents and I live on Oak Street. _____ like our apartment.

2. My mother's name is Elena. _____ is a librarian.

3. My father's name is Hector. _____ is a nurse.

4. My sisters' names are Maria and Alma. _____ are twins.

5. My family has a new car. _____ is blue.

6. I like to play soccer. What do _____ like to do?

car:

PRACTICE 4:
Read the question. Complete the answer.

1. Do you have any brothers or sisters?   Yes, _____ have two sisters.

2. Do your sisters go to your school?   Yes, _____ are in 1st grade.

3. Is your mother at school?   Yes, _____ is a librarian.

4. Is your father a teacher?   No, _____ is a nurse.

5. Is your car red?   No, _____ is blue.

PRACTICE 5:
Read. Write the correct word.

I'm Maria's son. Maria is _____my_____ mother.
<u>I / my</u>

1. Grandmother's name is Anna. ____ loves _____ daughter, Maria.
<u>She / Her</u>   <u>she / her</u>

2. My brother works in a library. _____ name is Juan.
<u>He / His</u>

3. I go to Harrison School. _____ like _____ teachers.
<u>I / My</u>   <u>I / my</u>

4. _____ help _____ parents every day.
<u>We / Our</u>   <u>we / our</u>

5. Who is in your family? What are _____ names?
<u>they / their</u>

PRACTICE 6:
Match. Write the form on the line.

he's   it's   they're   you're
I'm   she's   we're

you are _____*you're*_____

1. he is _____

2. she is _____

3. it is _____

4. we are _____

5. they are _____

6. I am _____

PRACTICE 7:
Write the word.

am   is   are

1. I _____ a student at Millington Central.

2. I _____ in the band at Millington Central.

3. Neville and Derek _____ in the band too.

4. We _____ friends.

5. Neville _____ on the basketball team, but Derek _____ not.

6. Derek's father _____ a music teacher at Millington Central.

7. He _____ also a math teacher.

8. _____ you in the band at your school?

G **PRACTICE 8:**
Read. Write the correct word or words.

is   aren't   I'm not
isn't   are   I am

A: Is this your hat?

B: Yes, it ____*is*____ .

hat:

1. A: Is Mr. Brown your teacher?
   B: No, he _____ .

2. A: Are these Tom's books?
   B: Yes, they _____ .

3. A: Are you Raymond's sister?
   B: No, _____ .

4. A: Are you a soccer player?
   B: Yes, _____ .

5. A: Are the pencils on the table?
   B: No, they _____ .

G PRACTICE 9:
Read. Write the correct words.

Are they	Are you	Am I
Is he	Is it	Is she

A: ___*Is she*___ at school?

B: Yes, she is.

1. A: _____ Mr. Perry?

   B: No, he is Mr. Johnston.

2. A: _____ a student?

   B: Yes, I am.

3. A: _____ in the band?

   B: No, I'm not.

4. A: _____ in your English class?

   B: Yes, she is.

5. A: _____ on the table?

   B: No, it isn't.

6. A: _____ your parents?

   B: Yes, they are.

 PRACTICE 10:
Listen. Circle the word.

Ahmed

Mahmud	**mother**	(**father**)	**sister**
1. Samira	**father**	**brother**	**mother**
2. Nassir	**sister**	**father**	**brother**
3. Ahmed	**daughter**	**son**	**father**
4. Fatima	**mother**	**sister**	**father**

Karen Carter is 16 years old. Her father's name is Carl. He is 41. Her mother's name is Judith. She is 44. Karen has a brother named Craig and a sister named Beth. Craig is 15, and Beth is 8. The Carters live at 911 Water Street in Chicago, Illinois. Their phone number is (312) 555–4071.

Woodside School District
Information Card

The _____ Family   Age: _____
Father's Name: _____   Age: _____
Mother's Name: _____   Age: _____
Children—Name: _____   Age: _____
Name: _____   Age: _____
Name: _____
Address: _____
_____
Phone: _____

✒️ **PRACTICE 12:**
Write about your family.

_____

_____

_____

_____

_____

_____

_____

_____

_____

A. Write the correct word under each picture in the family tree.

brother   father   grandfather   grandmother
mother   parents   sister

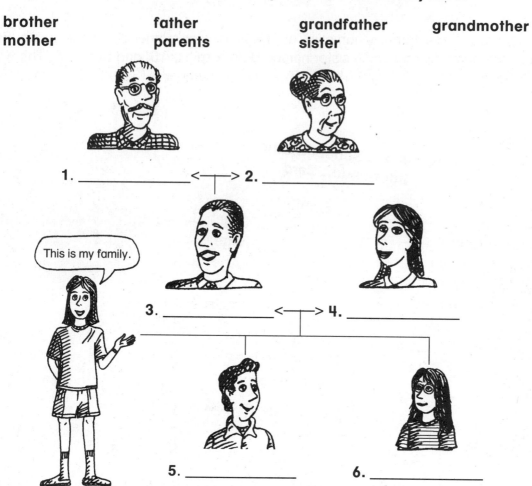

1. _____ <—┬—> 2. _____

This is my family.

3. _____ <—┬—> 4. _____

5. _____   6. _____

B. Read Alex's first letter to Pablo. Write the correct word.

Dear Pablo,

How (1.) _____ you? (2.) _____ name
  ~~is/are~~   ~~I/My~~

(3.) _____ Alex. I (4.) _____ 15 years old.
  ~~is/are~~   ~~are/am~~

(5.) _____ favorite class (6.) _____ science.
  ~~I/My~~   ~~is/are~~

(7.) _____ have two sisters. (8.) _____
  ~~I/She~~   ~~They/Their~~

names (9.) _____ Sofia and Yelena.
        ~~is/are~~

C. Complete the sentences about yourself and your family.

My name _____ . I _____ years old. My favorite

class _____ . I have _____ .

UNIT 7 At the Doctor's Office

PRACTICE 1:

Match. Write the letter on the line.

1. _____ He's happy.

2. _____ She's sick.

3. _____ He feels terrible.

4. _____ They're tired.

5. _____ They're thirsty.

6. _____ He's hungry.

7. _____ She's sad.

a.

b.

c.

d.

e.

f.

g.

PRACTICE 2:
Match. Write the letter on the line.

1. _____ finger

2. _____ toe

3. _____ stomach

4. _____ back

5. _____ head

6. _____ arm

7. _____ foot

8. _____ hand

9. _____ leg

10. _____ throat

PRACTICE 3:
Complete the sentences. Use these words.

hurts	sore	headache	stomachache	backache

1.

His stomach _____ . He has a _____ .

2.

She has a _____ arm. Her arm _____ .

3.

Her back _____ . She has a _____ .

4.

He has a _____ throat. His throat _____ .

5.

Her toe _____ . She has a _____ toe.

6.

His head _____ . He has a _____ .

PRACTICE 4:
Look at the picture. Write a sentence. Use <u>can</u> or <u>can't</u> and one of these action words.

cook   draw   kick   walk   play baseball   play the guitar

He can kick the ball.

1. _____

2. _____

3. _____

4. _____

5. _____

PRACTICE 5:
Answer the questions. Write <u>Yes, I can.</u> or <u>No, I can't.</u>

1. Can you play baseball? _____

2. Can you count to 100 in English? _____

3. Can you cook? _____

4. Can you sing? _____

PRACTICE 6:
Write questions and answers. Use <u>can</u> or <u>can't</u>.

A: Can he cook?

B: No, he can't.

1. A: _____

  B: _____

2. A: _____

  B: _____

3. A: _____

  B: _____

4. A: _____

  B: _____

PRACTICE 7:
Complete the sentences about you and the people in your family.

1. I can _____ .

2. I can't _____ .

3. My mother can _____ .

4. My _____ can't _____ .

5. My _____ can _____ .

6. My _____ can't _____ .

 PRACTICE 8:
Listen. Circle the answer to the question you hear.

1.
   a. Daniel is with his doctor.   **b.** Daniel is with his teacher.

2.
   a. Daniel feels great.   **b.** Daniel feels terrible.

3.
   a. Daniel has a stomachache.   **b.** Daniel has a sore foot.

4.
   a. Daniel has a sore throat too.   **b.** Daniel has a headache too.

5.
   a. Daniel feels tired.   **b.** Daniel is thirsty.

6.
   a. He has a backache.   **b.** He has the stomach flu.

7.
   a. Daniel needs to take medicine.   **b.** Daniel needs to go to the doctor
                                  on Tuesday.

PRACTICE 9:
Read about Tina. Answer the questions. Write sentences.

MEDICAL FORM

Name: _Tina_ _Anderson_
      First   Last

Address: _332 Concord Avenue_
         Street

Palo Alto   _California_   _94303_
  City   State   Zip Code

Phone Number: _(415) 555-9912_

Doctor's Name: _Dr. Ana Martinez_
Reason for seeing the doctor: _sore throat_

1. What is Tina's last name? _____
2. What city does she live in? _____
3. What is her zip code? _____
4. What is her doctor's name? _____
5. What is her reason for seeing the doctor? _____

PRACTICE 10:
Read about Tina. Pretend you are at the doctor's office. Write about yourself.

My name is Tina Anderson. My address is 332 Concord Avenue, Palo Alto, California 94303. My phone number is (415) 555-9912. My doctor's name is Dr. Ana Martínez. I am seeing the doctor because I have a sore throat.

_____
_____
_____
_____

A. Write the correct word on the line by each body part.

arm	back	finger	foot	hand
head	leg	stomach	throat	toe

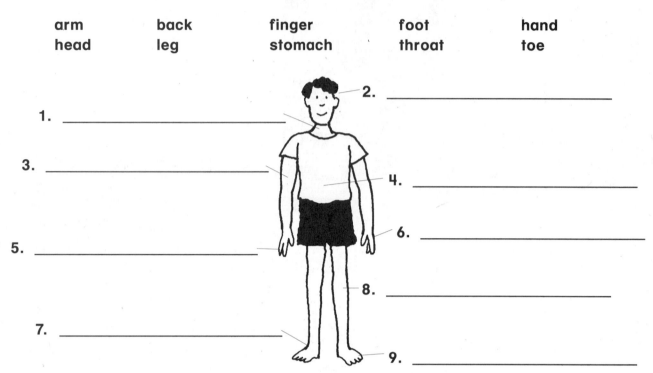

1. _____

2. _____

3. _____

4. _____

5. _____

6. _____

7. _____

8. _____

9. _____

B. Read Tony's medical form. Then complete the paragraph about him.

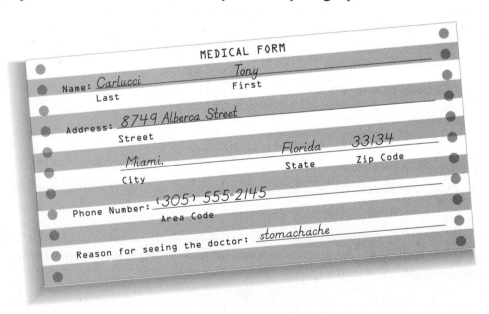

MEDICAL FORM

Name: _Carlucci_ _____ _Tony_ _____
Last   First

Address: _8749 Alberca Street_ _____
Street

Miami, _____ _Florida_ ___ _33134_ ____
City   State   Zip Code

Phone Number: _(305) 555-2145_ _____
Area Code

Reason for seeing the doctor: _stomachache_ _____

Tony is sick. He has a **(1)** _____ He can't go to school today, and he **(2)** _____ play soccer. He is at the doctor's office. A nurse is filling out a medical **(3)** _____ for him. His address is **(4)** _____ _____ . His phone number is **(5)** _____ .

PRACTICE 1:

Match the picture to the word. Write the letter on the line.

1. _____ supermarket

a.

2. _____ drugstore

b.

3. _____ post office

c.

4. _____ fire station

d.

5. _____ school

e.

6. _____ hospital

f.

7. _____ bank

g.

8. _____ police station

h.

PRACTICE 2:
Look at the map. Complete the sentence with the correct word. Use each word one time.

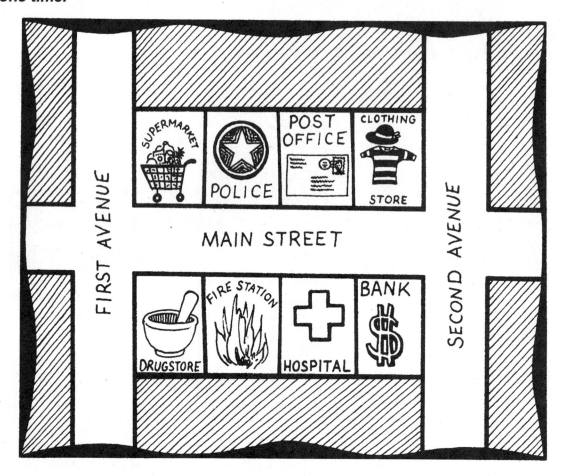

The _____*supermarket*_____ is next to the police station.

1. The _____ is between the drugstore and the hospital.

2. The _____ is between the police station and the clothing store.

3. The _____ is between the supermarket and the post office.

4. The _____ is between the bank and the fire station.

5. The _____ is next to the hospital.

6. The _____ is next to the fire station.

7. The _____ is next to the post office.

PRACTICE 3:
Circle the word or words for the sign.

 Phones. ⟨Stop.⟩ Go out here.

1. Don't go in. Go. Rest rooms.

2. Turn left. Don't turn left. Stop.

3. Rest rooms. Don't turn right. Phones.

4. Don't go in. Rest rooms. Go out here.

 PRACTICE 4:
Read. Circle the sign.

Don't walk.

1. Go out.

2. Phones.

3. Don't go in.

4. Don't go.

G PRACTICE 5:
Complete each sentence with _and_ or _or_.

I do homework on Saturday. I go to the park on Saturday.

I do homework ____*and*____ go to the park on Saturday.

1. I have computer class after lunch. I have math after lunch.

   I have computer class _____ math after lunch.

2. I have a pencil. I have paper.

   I have a pencil _____ paper.

3. My mother isn't a teacher. My mother isn't a librarian.

   My mother isn't a teacher _____ a librarian.

4. Walk past the bank. Walk past the fire station.

   Walk past the bank _____ the fire station.

5. Was she at the post office? Was she at the library?

   Was she at the post office _____ the library?

6. Do I turn at the fire station? Do I turn at the bank?

   Do I turn at the fire station _____ at the bank?

next to   **across from**   **past**   **between**

The store is _____*across from*_____ the park.

1. The park is _____ the police station.

2. The store is _____ the school.

3. The school is _____ the bank and the store.

4. The police station is _____ the bank.

5. The bank is _____ the school.

6. The school is _____ the park.

PRACTICE 7:
The X shows where Fernando lives. Listen. Draw a line on the map to show where he goes.

PRACTICE 8:
Look at the map. Circle <u>yes</u> or <u>no</u> to answer the questions.

Does Fernando go past the bank?   (yes)   no

1. Does Fernando walk past the school?   yes   no
2. Does Fernando turn right on Monroe Street?   yes   no
3. Does Fernando walk past the supermarket?   yes   no
4. Does Fernando walk about five blocks?   yes   no
5. Does Fernando go to the bookstore?   yes   no

PRACTICE 9:
Look at the map on page 62. Read Fernando's directions to get from the supermarket to the library. Draw a line to show his directions.

Turn right on Madison Street.

Go one block and turn right on Eighth Avenue.

Go past the fire station and the parking garage.

Turn left on Washington Street.

Go one block.

The library is on the corner of Washington and Ninth.

PRACTICE 10:
Answer the questions about Fernando's directions. Write complete sentences.

1. Does Fernando turn right on Madison Street or Monroe Street?

   _____

2. Does he go past the park or the parking garage?

   _____

3. From Eighth Avenue, does he turn right or left on Washington Street?

   _____

4. Is the library on the corner of Washington Street and Eighth Avenue or Washington and Ninth Avenue?

   _____

PRACTICE 11:
Look at the map on page 62. Complete the paragraph with the correct words.

To go from the supermarket to the park, go down Seventh **(1)** _____ to Jefferson School and turn **(2)** _____ on **(3)** _____ Street. Go **(4)** _____ blocks, and cross **(5)** _____ Avenue. The park is on the corner of **(6)** _____ Avenue and **(7)** _____ Street.

PRACTICE 12:
Look at the map on page 62. On a sheet of paper, write directions from the library to the school.

A. Use the map to answer the questions. Write the correct words.

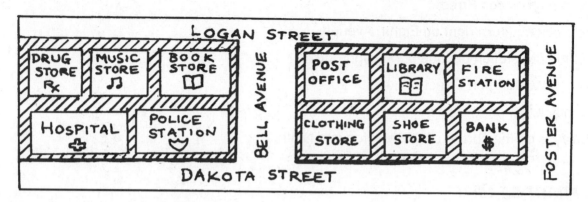

1. You are on the corner of Dakota and Foster. What building are you next to?

   _____

2. You are at the building between the post office and the fire station. Where are you?

   _____

3. You are at a building on Dakota Street. The building is next to the police station. Where are you?

   _____

4. You are at the drugstore. Do you turn right or left to go to the bookstore?

   _____

5. You are at the post office on Logan Street. Then you go past Bell Avenue to the second building

   on the left. Where are you? _____

B. Complete the paragraph with the correct words. Use the map.

To go from the drugstore to the shoe store, go **(1)** _____ block to Bell Avenue.

Turn **(2)** _____ on Bell Avenue. Go to **(3)** _____ Street and turn

(4) _____. The **(5)** _____ is the second store on your left.

C. Write directions on how to get from the bank to the bookstore.

_____

_____

_____

_____

_____

PRACTICE 1:
Look at the picture. Complete the sentence with the correct word.

bus driver	dentist	doctor	firefighter
librarian	mail carrier	police officer	salesperson

1. He's a _____ .

2. She's a _____ .

3. He's a _____ .

4. She's a _____ .

5. He's a _____ .

6. She wants to be a _____ .

7. He wants to be a _____ .

8. She wants to be a _____ .

PRACTICE 2:
Complete each sentence with the correct verb.

delivers	drives	fixes	helps
keeps order	picks up	puts out	sells

1. A police officer _____ .

2. A nurse _____ sick people.

3. A dentist _____ people's teeth.

4. A bus driver _____ a bus.

5. A mail carrier _____ and _____ people's mail.

6. A firefighter _____ fires.

7. A salesperson _____ things in a store.

PRACTICE 3:
Read. Write the correct word.

1. A doctor works at a _____ .
   library / hospital

2. A principal works at a _____ .
   school / store

3. A librarian works with _____ .
   teeth / books

4. A salesperson works in a _____ .
   store / fire station

5. A mail carrier delivers _____ .
   mail / chairs

PRACTICE 4:
Write the plural form of these nouns.

1. librarian _____

2. nurse _____

3. post office _____

4. fire station _____

5. supermarket _____

6. police station _____

7. dentist _____

8. salesperson _____

PRACTICE 5:
Complete the sentence. Write the plural form of the word.

firefighter	mail carrier	teacher
doctor	police officer	bus driver

1. _____ deliver mail to towns and cities.

2. _____ put out fires.

3. Harold and Rita take care of sick people. They are _____

4. _____ work in schools.

5. John and Rosa keep order. They are _____ .

6. _____ take people to where they want to go.

PRACTICE 6:
Complete the sentence by writing a form of <u>like</u> and <u>the infinitive</u> of one of these words. The words may be used more than once.

draw	go	listen	play
read	talk	write	

Carl _____*likes to draw*_____ airplanes.

1. Marvin _____ to school.

2. Maya and Sophia _____ basketball.

3. Anna _____ to music.

4. Bill _____ books.

5. Diana _____ to her teacher.

6. Fernando _____ letters to his friends.

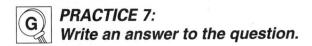

PRACTICE 7:
Write an answer to the question.

1. What do you like to do?

   _____

2. What don't you like to do?

   _____

3. Talk to a classmate. What does your classmate like to do?

   _____

4. What doesn't your classmate like to do?

   _____

PRACTICE 8:
Read the sentence. Write an answer.

1. Junko has a pen and some paper. What does she want to do?

   _____

2. Leander likes books. What does he want to be?

   _____

3. Elizabeth and Leah have a basketball. What do they want to do?

   _____

4. Anne Marie likes to help people learn. What does she want to be?

   _____

5. Yuri likes to draw. What class does he want to go to?

   _____

PRACTICE 9:
Read the question. Write an answer with <u>because</u>.

Why does Rose want to be a librarian?
She wants to be a librarian because she likes books.

1. Why does Mina want to be a police officer?

_____

2. Why does David want to go to the park?

_____

3. Why does Luis want to go to the gym?

_____

4. Why does Yelena want to be a doctor?

_____

5. Why does Jacques want to be a teacher?

_____

PRACTICE 10:
Listen to each sentence. Circle <u>T</u> for true and <u>F</u> for false for each sentence.

    (T)   F

1.	T F		5.	T F
2.	T F		6.	T F
3.	T F		7.	T F
4.	T F			

PRACTICE 11:
Read about David, his family, and their occupations. Then complete the chart.

My name is David Barret. My mother is a teacher. She likes her job because she likes to help students learn. My father is a librarian. He likes his work because he likes people and books. I want to be a firefighter because I want to help people.

Name	Occupation	Reason for Liking the Occupation
Mrs. Barret		
Mr. Barret		
David		

PRACTICE 12:
Fill in the chart about three people you know.

Name	Occupation	Reason for Liking the Occupation

PRACTICE 13:
Write about the people in your chart in Practice 12. Tell why they like their occupations.

_____

_____

_____

_____

_____

A. Complete the sentence with the correct occupation word and verb.

bus driver	dentist	firefighter	mail carrier	salesperson
delivers	drives	fixes	puts out	sells

1. A _____ _____ a bus.

2. A _____ _____ mail to people.

3. A _____ _____ teeth.

4. A _____ _____ things in a store.

5. A _____ _____ fires.

B. Read about Ramón and Lucy. Answer the questions. Use complete sentences.

Ramón wants to be a firefighter because he likes to help people. He also wants to put out fires. His friend Lucy wants to be a science teacher because science is her favorite class, and she likes to help other students learn.

1. What does Lucy want to be?

   _____

2. Why does she like this occupation?

   _____

3. What does Ramón want to be?

   _____

4. Why does he like this occupation?

   _____

C. What do you want to be? Why? Write your answers in complete sentences.

_____

_____

_____

apple juice	cheeseburger	French fries	fried chicken	hot dog
milk	pizza	salad	soup	

1. I'd like some _____ .

2. Jan would like a _____ .

3. Ted wants some _____ .

4. I'd like a _____ .

5. Pat wants a _____ .

6. Ali wants some _____ .

7. I'd like some _____ .

8. Sara would like some _____ .

9. Bob wants some _____ .

PRACTICE 2:
Look at the picture. Match the letter of the food with the sentence.

1. _____ I want a hamburger.

2. _____ I'd like some apple juice.

3. _____ I want some French fries.

4. _____ I want some fried chicken.

5. _____ I'd like a hot dog.

6. _____ I'd like some salad.

7. _____ I want a chicken sandwich.

8. _____ I'd like some milk.

PRACTICE 3:
Listen. Circle the amount you hear.

1. $3.10 $2.97 $20.90

2. $.25 $25.00 $20.05

3. $10.34 $4.30 $1.20

4. $5.89 $4.92 $9.42

5. $.49 $.97 $.38

6. $12.50 $12.05 $20.50

7. $10.42 $2.44 $1.24

8. $.75 $1.78 $5.73

 PRACTICE 4:
Write the amount of money on the line.

three dollars and twenty cents   _$3.20_

1. four dollars and fifty cents   _____

2. seventy-five cents   _____

3. two dollars and sixty-eight cents   _____

4. twenty-five dollars and fifty-nine cents   _____

5. forty-three cents   _____

6. eleven dollars and thirty-five cents   _____

PRACTICE 5:
Read the people's orders. Write a, an, or some on the line.

TRACY: I'd like **(1)** _____ vegetable soup and **(2)** _____ chicken sandwich.

SENG: I'd like **(3)** _____ hot dog and **(4)** _____ apple.

MARTA: I'd like **(5)** _____ cheeseburger and **(6)** _____ carton of milk.

NASSIR: I'd like **(7)** _____ piece of fried chicken and **(8)** _____ French fries.

OLGA: I'd like **(9)** _____ chicken soup, **(10)** _____ slice of pizza, and

(11) _____ apple juice.

RON: I'd like **(12)** _____ apple, **(13)** _____ piece of cheese, and

(14) _____ milk.

PRACTICE 6:
Write a, some, or any on the line.

1. Would you like _____ French fries?

2. Does Alexandra want _____ bowl of soup?

3. We don't have _____ French fries.

4. Would you like _____ pizza or _____ hot dog?

5. Does Ed want _____ apple juice with his lunch?

6. We don't have _____ fried chicken, but we have _____ chicken soup.

7. Does he want _____ soup and _____ cheese sandwich?

8. Would you like _____ slice of pizza or _____ fried chicken?

@@

PRACTICE 7:
Read the question. Write the answer on the line.

Does Maria have lunch at 12 o'clock?   Yes, _____*she does*_____ .

1. Do you like apple juice?   No, _____ .

2. Does Tim like pizza?   Yes, _____ .

3. Do they want some soup?   Yes, _____ .

4. Does Anna want some pizza?   No, _____ .

5. Do you and Sue like French fries?   Yes, _____ .

6. Does Sue want a hamburger with her French fries?   Yes, _____ .

7. Does Pierre want a cheese sandwich?   No, _____ .

PRACTICE 8:
Read the question. Write the answers to numbers 1 – 3 about yourself. Write the answers to numbers 4 – 8 about another person.

Do you like pizza?   _____*Yes, I do.*_____

1. Do you like fried chicken?   _____

2. Do you like vegetable soup?   _____

3. Do you like apple juice?   _____

4. Does _____ like milk?   _____
        (name)

5. Does _____ like hamburgers?   _____
        (name)

6. Does _____ like salad?   _____
        (name)

7. Does _____ like hot dogs?   _____
        (name)

8. Does _____ like pizza?   _____
        (name)

Ⓖ **PRACTICE 9:**
Complete the question and answer. Write <u>do</u> or <u>does</u> on the line.

1. A: _____ Lena want some pizza?

   B: Yes, she _____ .

2. A: _____ you want a hot dog?

   B: Yes, I _____ .

3. A: _____ Leroy want some French fries?

   B: Yes, he _____ .

4. A: _____ Matt and Pat want some milk?

   B: Yes, they _____ .

5. A: _____ your mother want to go to a restaurant?

   B: Yes, she _____ .

6. A: _____ you and Tony want hot dogs?

   B: Yes, we _____ .

PRACTICE 10:
Listen to the conversations. What does each person want? How much does it cost? Fill in the chart.

Food	$
1.	
2.	
3.	
4.	

PRACTICE 11:
Read about Alexandra and Ed. Use the menu to answer the questions.

ALEXANDRA: I want a chicken sandwich, a large green salad, and some milk, please.

ED: I'd like a hamburger, a small order of French fries, and apple juice, please.

Menu

hamburger	$1.99	French fries	large $1.15
			small .95
cheeseburger	2.29	salad	large 1.69
			small 1.19
chicken sandwich	1.89		
		carton of milk	.59
cheese sandwich	1.39	apple juice	.55

1. What does Alexandra want for lunch?

_____ $ _____

_____ $ _____

_____ $ _____

Total $ _____

2. What does Ed want for lunch?

_____ $ _____

_____ $ _____

_____ $ _____

Total $ _____

PRACTICE 12:
You have $4.25. Choose your lunch from the menu above. Write the names and the amounts. Write the total.

_____ $ _____

_____ $ _____

_____ $ _____

Total $ _____

PRACTICE 13:
Look at Practice 12. What do you want for lunch? How much is it? Write sentences.

_____

_____

A. Look at the picture. Complete the sentence with the correct words.

apple	apple juice	chicken soup	French fries
fried chicken	hamburger	pizza	salad

1. I'd like a _____ and some _____.

2. Luisa wants some _____ and an _____.

3. We'd like some cheese _____ and some _____.

4. Tony wants two pieces of _____ and a small _____.

B. Read the conversations. Write <u>a</u>, <u>some</u>, or <u>any</u> on the line.

1. A: Do you have _____ chicken sandwiches?

   B: No, we don't have _____ chicken sandwiches, but we have _____ hamburgers.

2. A: Do you have _____ soup?

   B: Yes, we have _____ chicken soup.

3. A: Would you like _____ hot dog?

   B: Yes, I'd like _____ hot dog and _____ French fries, please.

C. Read the menu. Choose three food items. Complete the sentence with your order. Then write the total.

hamburger	$1.99	French fries		milk	$.55
cheeseburger	2.19	large	$1.15	apple juice	.55
hot dog	1.29	small	.95		

I'd like _____.

TOTAL: $ _____

PRACTICE 1:
Look at the picture. Circle the word or words.

1. running   swimming   studying

2. playing football   playing basketball   riding a bike

3. swimming   skating   kicking a ball

4. kicking a ball   studying   writing letters

5. throwing a ball   hitting a ball   skating

6. skating   playing soccer   playing baseball

7. playing baseball   kicking a ball   doing homework

8. swimming   running   riding a bike

PRACTICE 2:
Match. Write the letter on the line.

1. _____ Mr. and Mrs. Carter are riding bikes.

a.

2. _____ Karen is running.

b.

3. _____ Ana and Barb are skating.

c.

4. _____ Carla is playing baseball with Dan.

d.

5. _____ Ken and Lin are playing Frisbee.

e.

6. _____ Ron and Eva are studying.

f.

7. _____ Susan is reading a book.

g.

PRACTICE 3:
Write anyone, everyone, no one, *or* someone *on the line.*

A: Is _____ *anyone* _____ riding a bike?

B: Yes, _____ *someone* _____ is riding a bike.

1. A: Is _____ skating in the park?

   B: Yes, _____ is skating in the park.

2. A: Is _____ catching the ball?

   B: No, _____ is catching the ball.

3. A: Is _____ swimming?

   B: Yes, _____ is swimming.

4. A: Is _____ riding a bike?

   B: Yes, _____ is riding a bike.

5. A: Is _____ kicking the soccer ball?

   B: Yes, _____ kicking the soccer ball?

6. A: Is _____ throwing a Frisbee?

   B: Yes, _____ is throwing a Frisbee.

7. A: Is _____ running?

   B: Yes, _____ is running.

8. A: Is _____ hitting the ball?

   B: No, _____ is hitting the ball.

PRACTICE 4:
Complete the sentence. Write _am_, _is_, or _are_ on the line.

Ron and Eva _____*are*_____ studying.

1. Luis _____ reading at home.

2. Carla and Barb _____ swimming in the pool.

3. I _____ throwing the baseball to Ana.

4. Rod and Ed _____ running with their friends.

5. Reiko _____ playing baseball with her friends.

6. Rosa and Susana _____ skating in the park.

G **PRACTICE 5:**
Read the question. Complete the answer on the line.

A: Is Juan studying English?

B: No, _____*he isn't*_____ .

1. A: Are Julie and Tomás playing basketball?

   B: Yes, _____ .

2. A: Is Elizabeth playing basketball?

   B: Yes, _____ .

3. A: Are Bao and Calvin running this afternoon?

   B: Yes, _____ .

4. A: Is Gretchen skating?

   B: No, _____ .

5. A: Are Nina and Allen riding bikes?

   B: No, _____ .

6. A: Is Sandra swimming?

   B: Yes, _____ .

7. A: Is Michael kicking the ball?

   B: No, _____ .

8. A: Are Mr. and Mrs. Santiago reading the paper?

   B: Yes, _____ .

PRACTICE 6:
Complete the question. Write the answer.

_____Are_____ Gloria and Susan working hard?   Yes, _____they are_____ .

1. _____ Teresa skating in the park?   No,_____ .

2. _____ the students sitting down?   Yes, _____ .

3. _____ Andrea opening the window?   No,_____ .

4. _____ the window open?   No,_____ .

5. _____ the students listening to the teacher?   Yes, _____ .

6. _____ the teacher reading her book?   No,_____ .

7. _____ Jean and Lewis answering their son?   Yes, _____ .

8. _____ Larry doing his homework?   Yes, _____ .

PRACTICE 7:
Look at the pictures and words. Ask and answer questions. Use <u>what</u> or <u>where</u> in each question.

TAKEO

A: What's Takeo doing?

B: He's studying in the library.

CARMEN

1. A: _____

   B: _____

DANNY AND KEVIN

2. A: _____

   B: _____

SUSAN

3. A: _____

   B: _____

MARK AND KARIM

4. A: _____

   B: _____

PRACTICE 8:
Listen. What is each person doing? Write the activity in the chart.

Name	Activity
1. Chung	*kicking a football*
2. Pedro	
3. Dave	
4. Anna	
5. Mom	

PRACTICE 9:
Read the letter. Answer the questions.

Dear María,
   Hi! How are you?
   I like my new school. I'm learning a lot of new things. I like to skate and write letters to my friends. I also like to play soccer with my sister Amy. She likes to swim too, but I don't like to swim. My brother Tom plays baseball at the park. Do you like to play baseball? I don't. What do you like to do?
   Please write me a letter soon.
                            Love, Linda

1. Who is writing the letter? _____

2. What can Linda do? _____

3. What does Linda like to do with her sister Amy? _____

4. What does Tom do at the park? _____

📖 **PRACTICE 10:**
Complete the charts about the people in Linda's letter.

Name	What do they like to do?
Amy	
Tom	

What does Linda like to do?	What doesn't Linda like to do?

📝 **PRACTICE 11:**
You are in a park. What are your friends doing? Write a letter to a friend or family member.

Dear _____,

_____

_____

_____

_____

_____

_____

A. What are the people doing? Write a sentence under each picture. Use He's, She's or They're and the action words in the list.

hitting a ball	swimming
running	riding bikes
kicking a ball	throwing a Frisbee

1. _____

2. _____

3. _____

4. _____

B. Read the letter. Answer the questions. Use complete sentences.

Dear Alicia,

    Everyone is at the park today. Isabel and Mayka are running. I want to swim, but the pool isn't open. That's why I'm writing this letter to you. What are you and your family doing? Can you go to the park with me on Saturday?

Your friend,

Carmen

1. Where is everyone? _____

2. What are Isabel and Mayka doing?_____

3. What does Carmen want to do? _____

4. What is Carmen doing? _____

C. You are Carmen. Write a letter to Alicia. Answer her questions.

_____

_____

_____

UNIT 12 At the Clothing Store

V **PRACTICE 1:**
Look at the picture. Write the word for each item of clothing.

jacket   jeans   shirt   shoes

skirt   sweater   T-shirt

1. _____

2. _____

3. _____

4. _____

5. _____

6. _____

7. _____

PRACTICE 2:
Match. Write the letter on the line.

1. _____ Diana's looking for shoes.

2. _____ The jeans cost $15.

3. _____ The shoes are too big for Katy.

4. _____ Lyn needs a new jacket.

5. _____ The T-shirt is too small for David.

6. _____ AJ's buying a shirt.

7. _____ Sara's buying a skirt.

PRACTICE 3:
Look at the amounts. Write the number of coins and dollars you need.

	$1.00	25¢	10¢	5¢	1¢
$1.61	1	2	1		1
1. $2.45					
2. $ .24					
3. $4.75					
4. $3.95					

PRACTICE 4:
Read the sentences. Write how much change you get.

Ten pencils cost $2.59. You give the salesperson $20.00.

Change: ___$17.41___

1. A notebook costs $2.99. You give the salesperson $5.00.

   Change: _____

2. A book costs $6.39. You give the salesperson $10.00.

   Change: _____

3. A pen costs $1.52. You give the salesperson $5.00.

   Change: _____

4. A desk is on sale for $59.99. You give the salesperson $60.00.

   Change: _____

5. Three erasers are on sale for $1.09. You give the salesperson $2.00.

   Change: _____

6. Paper is on sale for $2.33. You give the salesperson $10.00.

   Change: _____

7. Four books are on sale for $22.34. You give the salesperson $25.00.

   Change: _____

G **PRACTICE 5:**
Make a sentence out of the words. Write the sentence on the line.

shirt red this likes Bill   _Bill likes this red shirt_.

1. blue want I shoes these   _____.

2. brown this I to want buy jacket   _____.

3. likes the Ron shirt black   _____.

4. skirt long Lisa to this buy wants   _____.

G **PRACTICE 6:**
Complete each sentence. Choose any of the words from the chart.
Use each clothing word and color word one time.

this	~~jeans~~	black
these	shoes	~~blue~~
	socks	green
	sweater	red
	T-shirt	white

Alma wants   _these blue jeans_.

1. Ned likes   _____.

2. Elena likes   _____.

3. Jorge wants   _____.

4. I like   _____.

PRACTICE 7:
Listen. What are they buying?
Write the clothing items on the line.

a black jacket

1. _____

2. _____

3. _____

4. _____

PRACTICE 8:
Read about the clothes. Write the answers.

1. How much is the T-shirt? _____

2. What is the order number for the yellow T-shirt? _____

3. What are the sizes of the jeans? _____

4. How much does number 32 cost? _____

5. How much does a blue skirt cost? _____

6. What color is number 38? _____

SPRINGO

T-SHIRT $6.95 SIZES: S,M,L
COLORS   ORDER NUMBER:
green......28
yellow......29
blue......30

JEANS $19.95 SIZES: S,M,L
COLORS: ORDER NUMBER:
blue........31
black........32
green........35

SPRINGO

SHIRT $12.95 SIZES: S,M,L
COLORS: ORDER NUMBER:
Pink........34
white......35
orange......36

SKIRT $14.50 SIZES: S,M,L
COLORS   ORDER NUMBER:
yellow..........37
white..........38
blue..........39

PRACTICE 9:
Look at the catalog pages above.
Choose three clothing items.
Fill out the the form.

Springo Clothing Company

Name: _____
      Last   First

Address: _____
         Street

_____
    City   State   Zip Code

Phone Number: (   ) _____
          Area Code

Name of Item	Color	Order Number	How Many	Size	Cost
				Total	

PRACTICE 10:
Look at the form in Practice 9. What are you ordering? How much do the clothes cost? Write your answers in sentences.

_____

_____

_____

A. Look at the picture. Complete the sentence with the correct words.

| jacket | jeans | shirt | shoes | big | long |
| skirt | sweater | socks | T-shirt | short | small |

1. I'd like to buy these _____

   and _____ .

2. Rita is buying a black _____ and

   a white _____ .

3. This _____ is too _____ !

4. This _____ is too _____ !

5. Max doesn't want these _____ .

   They're too _____ !

B. Fill out the form with two clothing items.

Jeans $24.95
Sizes: 29, 30, 31, 32, 33
J1 - blue
J2 - black

Sweaters $21.95
Sizes: S, M, L
S4 - blue
S5 - red

Name of Item	Color	Order Number	How Many	Size	Cost
				Total	

C. What are you ordering? Answer with the clothing and color words from the form.

_____

_____